Puppy Training

The Complete Guide To Housebreak Your Puppy in Just 7 Days

Dan O'Brian

DAN O'BRIAN

© **Copyright 2016 by Dan O'Brian - All rights reserved.**

This document is geared towards providing exact and reliable information in regards to the topic and issue covered. The publication is sold with the idea that the publisher is not required to render accounting, officially permitted, or otherwise, qualified services. If advice is necessary, legal or professional, a practiced individual in the profession should be ordered.

- From a Declaration of Principles which was accepted and approved equally by a Committee of the American Bar Association and a Committee of Publishers and Associations.

In no way is it legal to reproduce, duplicate, or transmit any part of this document in either electronic means or in printed format. Recording of this publication is strictly prohibited and any storage of this document is not allowed unless with written permission from the publisher. All rights reserved.

The information provided herein is stated to be truthful and consistent, in that any liability, in terms of inattention or otherwise, by any usage or abuse of any policies, processes, or directions contained within is the solitary and utter responsibility of the recipient reader. Under no circumstances will any legal responsibility or blame be held against the publisher for any reparation, damages, or monetary loss due to the information herein, either directly or indirectly.

Respective authors own all copyrights not held by the publisher.

The information herein is offered for informational purposes solely, and is universal as so. The presentation of the information is without contract or any type of guarantee assurance.

The trademarks that are used are without any consent, and the publication of the trademark is without permission or backing by the trademark owner. All trademarks and brands within this book are for clarifying purposes only and are the owned by the owners themselves, not affiliated with this document.

INTRODUCTION

I want to thank you and congratulate you for purchasing the book, "Puppy Training - The Complete Guide To Housebreak Your Puppy in Just 7 Days".

This book has actionable steps and strategies on how to housebreak a puppy in just a week.

Owning a puppy is an amazing thing, as a puppy brings an incredible feeling of immense joy. In as much as having a puppy is a great experience, there are also challenges that come with owning a puppy. One of these challenges is house training. There is nothing exciting about finding your puppy always peeing on your sofa, carpets and anywhere possible you can think of. Hence, with owning a puppy comes the responsibility of house breaking the puppy and ensuring that they don't urinate everywhere in the house but in a specific designated area.

The thought of housebreaking a dog often makes many new puppy owners feel highly nervous and worried because house breaking a puppy is not an easy job. A lot goes into ensuring your dog pays heed to your instructions and always excretes in the designated area instead of littering everywhere in, and outside the house.

If you intend to housebreak your puppy but haven't been able to achieve any success, this book is the perfect match. This book is a definitive guide to house training your dog in just seven days. Yes, you read it right, 7 days. Follow this guide and you'll successfully train your puppy in a week.

Thanks again for purchasing this book, I hope you enjoy it!

TABLE OF CONTENTS

Introduction v

Understanding Your Puppy's Psychology viii

The Importance Of Crate Training In House Breaking 6

Day 1: Setting Your Puppy's Routine 8

Day 2: House Breaking A Puppy - A Few Don'ts, And How To Avoid Them 12

Day 3: Poop Patrol- Identifying Your Dog's Poop Signals 16

Day 4: Choosing The Right Training Method For Your Puppy ... 18

Day 5: Condition Your Puppy - The Magic Of Positive Reinforcement 24

Day 6: Using the Startle, But Never Scare Method 28

Day 7: Practice All That You Have Learned 30

Conclusion 32

MY FREE GIFT TO YOU! 34

Other Books by Dan O'Brian 38

UNDERSTANDING YOUR PUPPY'S PSYCHOLOGY

Before embarking on housetraining your puppy in seven days, you must make some effort to understand your puppy's psychology and know him or her better. This will make it easier to train him, or her ☺.

Let' start by doing that

Understanding Your Puppy

As a puppy/dog owner, you must:

Realize That A Puppy Is Like A Little Baby: The first thing you must understand is this; your puppy is still a baby; you cannot expect it to grasp everything you are saying or commanding from day one. Sure, a puppy is capable of doing a lot more compared to a human baby at eight weeks, but that doesn't mean the puppy is all grown up.

You have brought him into your house, which is a comforting place for you, but an entirely new environment for him. At first, your puppy will feel strange and might not respond to you in an affectionate manner from day one. This is why you need to give the puppy time to adjust to the new environment.

Show love and care to your furry baby to make it feel welcomed and loved. This will help the puppy understand that you are a loving owner and think only what is best for it, which will end up making it easier for your puppy to follow your instructions.

Don't Delay the Process: Even though you should give your puppy about a week to settle into the new environment, you must not delay the housebreaking process. You may think it is best to train the dog when it grows older since it's only a baby now and you would have to give it a great amount of time. However sound this approach sounds, it is wrong.

Until he or she becomes 12 weeks old, puppies do not have control over the muscle that lets it hold pee; if you don't make haste to train your puppy to pee and poop outside, or in a set location in the house, it is going to defecate all over your house. Your rug will smell of pee, and your favorite reading spot will be soiled with poop, and the more a place smells like pee, the more the puppy will urinate here because they associate the area with pee.

Understand Mother Nature: Housebreaking a dog is relatively simple when you understand Mother Nature. Similar to how mothers' potty train children at a certain age, a dog also trains her kids to excrete outside, or next to their pen whenever she feels her pups need to excrete.

After birth, puppies normally eat and excrete inside the den. The mother notices this act and cleans all the mess to ensure the filthy odor does not remain on her pups, or in the den. As they grow, she starts nudging them to go outside the den to excrete. With time, they learn to excrete far from the den. This shows that it is in a dog's nature to excrete outside their place of residence. In your case, the only difference is that you will play the role of your puppy's mother; therefore, it is your duty to train him.

Know the Dog's Nature: Another important thing you must comprehend prior to starting the seven-day plan is your dog's nature. This entails two things: the breed and needs of your puppy, and the dog's nature to please the master.

Dog's Breed: Each dog is different and belongs to a specific breed. Every breed has its own set of needs and requirements, and behaves in a certain manner. Before beginning the housebreaking process, you must completely understand your dog; understand what he likes to eat, how much it eats, how many times it urinates and poops, how its digestive system works, and how long it takes him to excrete after a meal. This information will accordingly help you train your dog, and enable you to create a routine that suits both, you and your furry little friend.

Dogs Love to Please: The second thing you must bear in mind is that it is in every dog's nature to please the master. Dogs don't like it when you, the master, is upset; thus, a dog always wants to do things that please the master.

It is likely your puppy will exhibit the same behavior. It will become upset upon seeing you angry, and will run towards you and show signs of excitement when you smile at him. You must learn to make the best use of this in-built dog behavior and use it to your advantage.

Observe your dog closely to show resentment towards his poor behavior such as peeing inside the house, so he knows that this act has made you angry.

Accompany Your Puppy Everywhere: If you see him peeing on the rug, but take five to six minutes to show your disapproval, the puppy will think you are upset because of the mess on the floor and not the act of relieving himself on the rug. Therefore, he will continue with this practice and will become sad and confused upon seeing you infuriated, but won't understand the problem.

Ensure to accompany your dog everywhere during the first few days of its arrival in your home. Follow him wherever he goes, so you can promptly show your resentment if you find him excreting inside the house. This helps the pup understand the reason behind your resentment, which, with your guidance of course, helps him gradually eliminate this behavior to please you.

Let's swiftly move on to the next section.

Puppy Owner's Manual: Figuring Out If You're Ready Or Not

As much as it is important to understand your dog's psychology and determine the ideal time to train him, you also need to figure out whether or not you ready to venture into the housebreaking process.

As a dog owner, you're responsible for training your dog and make it follow rules so it never leaves puddles of urine and bundles of poop everywhere in your house. Therefore, it is imperative to get some insight into your routine, needs, and psychology as well, so you can begin this process at the right time.

How to Know If you're ready to start the House Training Process

As we indicated earlier, housetraining your puppy is not a walk in the park. It requires a lot of dedication, time, and commitment. In this regard, you must prepare yourself and ensure you're ready to embark on the training. How do you know, or how can you tell if you're ready? You're ready if:

You Have Sufficient Time: Housebreaking a little pup means following him wherever he moves. If he goes into the bathroom, you must follow it; if you find it sneaking into the kitchen, you need to run after it.

You need to be on your toes the entire time your puppy is moving around; this is important so you can examine the pups behavior, know when it excretes, and show it resentment promptly if it poops in the house. Therefore, housebreaking a puppy is a hectic job and one that demands you to invest a great amount of time. Therefore, you must begin this process when you have sufficient time at your disposal.

This doesn't mean you have to stop working, or take a seven day leave from the office. It merely means you must be ready to give proper time and care to your pup once you reach home from work; and if you don't work, then you must be prepared to invest a portion of time to training your dog.

If you have a big office presentation or project coming up, or have to prepare for your wedding, then it is best to postpone dog training for a few days and begin this process once you are through with the hectic and time-consuming jobs; this will allow you to focus entirely on puppy training once you get started.

Are Ready to Stay Alert and Active: The housebreaking process demands that you stay active and alert. This allows you to observe your dog and notice the different pee or poop indicators it portrays.

Prepare your mind and body to remain attentive and energetic once you start with this process. You don't need to increase your daily caffeine intake to stay alert 24/7 because too much caffeine is bad. However, you can drink herbal teas, such as ginseng and rhodiola rosea teas to stay energetic. Studies show that both these teas can help combat fatigue and improve your energy levels.

Are Ready To Calm Yourself And Remain Calm: Often**,** new dog owners experience nervousness when housebreaking a dog; they lose their calm when they see the dog peeing on their favorite couch and start shouting at the dog. This stresses the dog, often making it experience depression. To properly house train your dog, you need to remain calm and always stay in a relaxed, cool mood.

Sure, it infuriates you when your pup fails to understand a signal or follow your command. Irrespective of how much truth that statement holds, the right way to make a pup understand your displeasure is to show resentment via your expressions and not your voice. Before you begin training your dog to excrete in a designated area, spend some time training yourself to stay cool and calm with your furry friend. Tell yourself that this process isn't an easy one, but with time and patience, you'll definitely get there.

Be patient with your pup and give him your love and support so he or she can pick on the cues and commands easily, and follow them conveniently. To stay calm, practice deep breathing and resort to this practice every time you are angry with the puppy.

THE IMPORTANCE OF CRATE TRAINING IN HOUSE BREAKING

Before we can move on to learn about house breaking, it is important to look at crate training. Crate training is important since you need to find a permanent home for your puppy, which in this case would be the crate. Furthermore, since dogs don't usually like excreting where they sleep, crate training your dog will ensure that the puppy gets used to their crate as their home and does not defecate in their crate but will wait for you to take them to the designated area. So how exactly do you crate train your puppy? Let us find out.

How Crate Training Works

Get a Suitable Crate: You need to purchase a crate for your dog according to his size and breed.

Next, place the crate in an area that most of the family members spend their time. The dog needs to feel like they are still people around and they are not in some room alone.

Make the Crate Comfortable: Add a few elements of comfort such as some toys or a comfortable blanket in the crate. This provides a comforting, welcoming environment for your pup encouraging him to enter the crate. You can also use treats and different positive reinforcement strategies to lure your dog into the crate.

Drain Him Off the Extra Energy: Before making your dog enter the crate, try making him exercise a little. This drains him off all the extra energy; he becomes relaxed when he has to enter the crate and doesn't make any fuss inside it.

Get Your Puppy: Get your puppy to come close to the crate and enter it. Use words like "enter pup" or "go in" to encourage the puppy to move into the crate. Do not try to drag the puppy into the crate, as this will make them see their crate as a bad place to be. It is important that the puppy gets in the crate alone. The treats that you put into the crate will serve as a way of getting your puppy into the crate.

Once your puppy enters the crate, allow them to find comfort in the crate and just as he does, gently close the door and sit close to the crate so your dog can see you and feel like they are not alone. Do not allow the puppy to stay in the crate for too long. The first time, you can let them stay in the crate for 30 minutes then over time, you can increase this time until they are comfortable being in the crate.

The sections that follow will outline an easy, seven-day process guaranteed to housetrain your puppy_ or any dog for that matter.

DAY 1: SETTING YOUR PUPPY'S ROUTINE

The last few sections have equipped you with an understanding of the basics of housebreaking your puppy; at this point, you're ready to begin the process.

The first day of the seven-day training and house breaking plan focuses on making efforts to set your dog's routine. Why is setting a routine for your dog the first thing you must do?

Importance Of Setting A Routine

When you set a proper routine for your puppy, you will ascertain that your dog eats at certain times, and excretes at specific times. Although there will be days when your pup will bring variations to your time, and will change his eating or pooping schedule a bit, the routine will more or less remain the same. This makes things easy for you because you will know when to direct your pup to move towards the excreting area, or go outside.

Moreover, setting your dog's routine makes life simple and easy for him. He gets his meals on time, and excretes accordingly. This will help his digestive system work smoothly and efficiently and experience less problems. Secondly, a routine will help your pup sleep on time every night and wake up fresh the next morning.

Pups who haven't become accustomed to pooping and urinating routinely often wake up several times from their sleep and wake up grumpy the next day. To ensure you, your family and puppy stay healthy and happy; your first priority needs to be setting a daily routine for your little friend.

Here's how you can accomplish this goal.

How To Set Your Pup's Routine

Setting a routine for your dog isn't difficult; it simply requires a little patience and care. The guidelines below will help you set a routine for your puppy.

Wake Your Pup at a Specific Time

The first thing to do when setting your pup's routine is to wake the pup at the same time daily. Ensure that this time is after you wake up daily so he does not wake up before you do and soil your room. If you wake up at around 8, make sure to wake your puppy at around 9. Right after you wake it up, give it a warm hug, and then take it to the specific area where it pees.

Walk the Dog

Once your puppy is fresh and awake, let it walk outside. Make sure not to carry it because it will make your pup accustomed to this habit and he would want you to pick him up and take him out every time. Start walking in front of your pup and ask it to follow you. Once your dog is outside, let it excrete in a certain area.

Feed Your Dog

After your puppy has finished excreting, let him accompany you inside and give it breakfast. It is essential to feed your pup at this time every single day. Give him a sufficient amount of the meal in the bowl and make sure to take it away once he is finished eating.

If your pup finds the bowl in the eating-place, or in their den, they are likely to eat from it every now and then. This would disturb their eating regimen, making them excrete repeatedly. Therefore, it is essential to feed your pup a specific amount of food at specific times of the day to ensure it does not excrete repeatedly.

Make sure your pup Naps Daily

Ensure your pup naps for an hour or two daily to ensure it's eating and excretion times remain aligned and consistent.

Set a Play Time

Setting a specific playtime is essential to your pup's wellbeing; it allows the pup to get a break from the monotonous routine, feel fresh and happy, and enjoy living with you.

Play with your pup for about one hour. This helps the two of you bond, bringing you and your pup closer, which makes it easier for him to consider you the master. The better bonded you and your pup are, the easier it will be for your pup to follow your instructions regarding housebreaking.

Schedule Consistent Excretion Times

Schedule consistent pooping and peeing times for your pup. To set excretion times for your pup, you must understand the pup's anatomy.

A dog excretes about four times daily, which makes it a bit difficult to train the pup in a few minutes. Therefore, when you let him out to poop or pee, give him sufficient time to do it.

A puppy normally defecates about five to thirty minutes after eating a meal. Keep this information in mind when setting the right excretion time for your pup. After properly feeding your puppy, make sure to take it out in the open after five to six minutes. Give the puppy forty minutes to wander around the 'elimination spot' so he can relax and defecate easily. Soon, this practice will start serving as a trigger for your pup, making it excrete easily. Make sure to take your dog to the exact same spot for defecating each time. This is important because your puppy starts becoming familiar to certain scents, places and areas, and when you take your pup to the same spot at a certain time frequently, it will know it needs to excrete. Keep these guidelines in mind and take your pup out three to four times a day to relieve according to its food intake.

Set a Sleep Time

Lastly, focus on setting sleep time for your pup so it sleeps at the same time daily and gets a good night's sleep and wakes up fresh and active the next morning.

Keep this procedure in mind and practice it with your dog on the first day to set its proper routine. This technique does not end on this day. You must continue with this routine for the remaining six days.

DAY 2: HOUSE BREAKING A PUPPY - A FEW DON'TS, AND HOW TO AVOID THEM

The first day taught you how to create a routine for your puppy so you can get him accustomed to the routine and let him know that he has to poop or pee at a specific time and at a designated area and not wherever he wants.

On the second day, you are going to reinforce learnings from the first day, and are going to focus on understanding some essential don'ts of housebreaking a dog.

Housetraining A Pup: Don'ts

There are certain do's of housebreaking a dog, such as setting up its routine and practicing positive reinforcement. Similarly, there are certain don'ts of this process as well.

These don'ts are there to help you understand things you must not do when potty training your dog. Avoiding these don'ts will ensure you train your dog the right way and don't upset him or her, or condition the dog to negative elements.

Below are things you **MUST NOT DO** when housetraining your pup:

Changing their Food Brand

When potty training, never change the brand of your dog's food, as sudden changes in the diet can upset your doggy's tummy, give the puppy diarrhea, and change the pup's excretion routine and timings.

Additionally, don't offer your dog any table scraps as it can fill his tummy too much, making it poop more than his usual routine.

Free Feeding

Free feeding is never a good idea, since it gives your dog the chance to eat as much as it wants and then poop as much as it wants and that too, at unpredictable times. This upsets the routine you worked so hard to create on day one.

Physical Punishment

If you find your dog excreting somewhere other than the set location, you must not throw any object at it, even if it is something soft as a wool ball. Punishment is not an effective method of training. Instead of encouraging your dog to follow the routine, it confuses your dog because it now thinks that they should not defecate and this can lead to greater health problems.

Dual Housebreaking

Decide whether to indoor train your dog, or outdoor housebreak them. Dual housebreaking is a big '**No No**'; it confuses the dog and often leads to stress. Pitts, a popular dog trainer based in California always advises his clients to practice either one of the two: outdoor or indoor elimination and then stick to that (more on these methods in later chapters).

Rubbing His Nose in Poop or Pee

According to various dog-training experts and the American Humane Association, rubbing a dog's nose in its mess is an abuse, and an unacceptable behavior. Your dog does not comprehend why you are doing this, and may start fearing and avoiding you.

Leaving Your Pup Unattended for a Long While

We have already established the need to be around your pup all the time when you are housebreaking it; do not leave your pup unattended. If you have to do something urgent while the pup is out in the open, run that errand fast, and return to your pup quickly.

Withholding Water from your Thirsty Dog

If you find your dog panting for water, give him the drink he needs. Never withhold water from your thirsty pup as a way of making him pee less, since just as you need water to survive, so does your dog.

On the second day, keep all these points in mind and avoid exercising them as you train your puppy. If you find yourself doing any of these actions, stop the moment you realize your mistake and take a few deep breaths. It is human to err but to train your dog correctly, ensure not to continue with these don'ts.

PUPPY TRAINING

DAY 3: POOP PATROL- IDENTIFYING YOUR DOG'S POOP SIGNALS

Well done! You are through with the first two days of the plan and that's a noteworthy achievement. On this day, you are going to practice an effective technique that will help you easily understand the excretion timings of your puppy.

Just like humans, dogs practice certain gestures and make some moves that signal that they want to excrete. You must learn how to look for, and identify such signs in your dog to understand him better and to know when he needs to relieve himself.

A three to four week pup won't be able to give any visible signs when he wants to pee because he cannot hold his pee; but a bigger pup will mostly give one or all of the following poop and pee signals. So, watch out for them.

Restlessness

Most dogs tend to become restless when they want to excrete. They start moving here and there, begin circling a certain spot and might even grasp hold of an object and tug it hard. If you observe these signs in your dog, then it is likely he wants to poop or pee.

Sniffing

Dogs become used to the smell of their toilet area after a few days and have the habit of sniffing it when they are eliminating. Therefore, if you find your dog incessantly sniffing the floor or anything else, it is probable they are telling you to take them out to their toilet spot, so they can defecate.

Door Scratching

Some dogs start scratching the door, or even bark at it when they want to go out to the toilet. If you see your dog doing the same, take it out so it can excrete and become calm.

Whine

Certain dogs start whining softly and then gradually increase their whine intensity when they want to relieve themselves. If you know your dog is well fed and isn't stressed out, but find him whining nonetheless, then it is likely that he wants to visit his toilet.

Poop and pee signals vary from one dog to another, but most dogs practice the aforementioned signals. You need to study your dog very closely and observe how he behaves just when he needs to excrete, so you can understand his toilet signal and pay heed to that sign promptly.

DAY 4: CHOOSING THE RIGHT TRAINING METHOD FOR YOUR PUPPY

On the fourth day, you are going to decide on one housetraining method for your pup and then stick to it. As stated earlier, there are two main housetraining methods: indoors or outdoors.

The indoor method has two tributary types. This chapter will she some light on the different housebreaking methods, along with the factors you need to consider when choosing a certain method, which will allow you to select the most appropriate method for your dog.

Indoors Vs. Outdoors Housebreaking: Which One Should You Use

Indoor housebreaking involves training your dog to excrete at a fixed spot inside the house. You use newspapers, or a litter pan to ensure your dog relieves him or herself at a particular indoors spot (we shall discuss these three methods in a while.)

Outdoor housetraining involves teaching and training your pup to defecate outdoors. You can use newspapers, litter pans etc for outdoor training, but generally, these tools are not a necessity in outdoor housebreaking.

Opt for outdoor housetraining if your dog is:

Large and excretes enormous piles and puddles, can easily use the doggie door, you can assist him or her get to the potty area outdoors and if there is an open area outside your house that is suitable for use for defecating.

However, if your pup is small and excretes small piles and puddles of poop and pee, or you have a hectic work schedule and cannot guide her outdoors regularly, or there isn't an appropriate potty area outside your house, or you want her to be trained indoors, then it is best to choose the indoor housebreaking method.

Using these tips, you can easily decide which of the two plans suit you and your puppy best. Let us discuss these plans individually.

Outdoor Housetraining

To begin outdoor housetraining, first choose a suitable area outdoors where your dog can pee and poop comfortably. Opt for an area with a big patch of soil. There must not be any wild plants, especially ones with thorns; also opt for a wide, open area.

Next, begin training your dog using the outdoor housetraining steps listed below:

Choose a Phrase that Tells Him to Go Excrete

You could select anything, such as 'go pee', 'go potty', 'go empty yourself', or anything else. Your dog will grow accustomed to these words and will soon follow their command. You can also use newspapers or a litter pan to make your dog excrete at a certain spot outdoors, but these tools seldom find use in the outdoors housebreaking method.

Figure Out Your Pup's Defecation Time

Next, figure out your dog's pee and poop time. You have been working on developing his routine, right. This is where that will come in handy. As you have most likely created your dog's routine, you can easily determine when your dog needs to excrete.

Often, dogs excrete when they wake up, after drinking or eating, and once during playtime. Once you have figured out your dog's excretion time, use the phrase you created earlier to command him to go out and pee.

To ensure your dog follows your command and goes outside to excrete, you could use the umbilical cord method, or dog door.

Let's look closely at these techniques.

The Umbilical Cord Method

The Umbilical cord method refers to keeping your dog attached to you all the time as a fetus attaches to its mother via an umbilical cord. In your case, a leash is going to act as the umbilical cord. Get a leash and attach it to your pup's collar. Fasten the leash to its pen or any other object whenever you don't want to hold it, and unfasten it to take hold of it when you want to take your dog outside to poop or pee.

When you're aware that your puppy needs to relieve himself, hold his leash and take him outside. Make sure, you make him walk. This method is suitable for you if you have sufficient time at your disposal and can spend that time with your dog, and if your dog likes being leashed. If your dog is not yet comfortable with the leash after a few days, then it is clear it doesn't like this method of training; you should instead try using the dog door.

Using the Dog Door

Some dog owners find it easy to use a dog door for housetraining their dogs. You can use the same tool if it suits you. Get a dog door relative to the size of your dog, and install it in your door.

Next, make your dog walk through the dog door whenever you find him signaling that he wants to excrete. During the first two to three days, you need to open the flap of the door yourself to ensure the flap doesn't hit and scare your puppy. In about two to three days, your pup will grow accustomed to this tool and will use it successfully. This method is suitable if you want your dog to become independent.

Let Your Pup Poop

Next, you need to let your pup go out and take time to relieve himself. Don't utter any word or give him a signal that shows he must hurry through the process. This will make him hold some of the pee inside, which will upset the routine.

Keep practicing this routine for the remaining four days and by the end of the seven days, your will have housetrained your pup. You must remember to use positive reinforcements when your puppy obeys a command and follows the routine properly (we'll look at positive reinforcement in subsequent chapters).

Indoor Housetraining

Indoor house training is most suitable for puppy owners who may live in apartments and don't necessarily have a backyard that the dog can use. The common indoor housetraining method is paper training. Let us look closely at this method.

Paper Training

Paper training is a popular indoor housetraining method wherein you use old newspapers to help your dog excrete in a fixed spot. In this method, you place a pile of old newspapers in any spot you wish for your puppy to use as an excretion point.

You must use the same spot each time to ensure your dog becomes used to excreting on paper and at a certain spot, and stops going to a different prohibited place each time. Moreover, paper absorbs feces and urine, making it easier for you to clean up, as you simply need to take the soiled paper and discard it. This method is extremely easy, simple, and cheap. You can also use puppy pads or litter pans for this method.

Litter pan training is the same as paper training, except that in litter pan training, you use a litter pan instead of newspapers to serve as your dog's toilet. Litter pans are available in supermarkets and stores that sell housebreaking tools and supplies.

How to Paper Train your Dog

This method is best for you if you don't want to spend extra on getting a pan for your pup and want a disposable technique. So how do you go about paper training your puppy?

Choosing a Spot

To begin paper-training your dog, decide on a spot that will serve as your pup's toilet. It is best to choose a small room or area you can confine using a puppy gate. Choose an area that has linoleum, tiled, or hardwood floor because these floors are easy to clean and don't soak up any urine.

Never opt for a carpeted area because the carpet will absorb the urine making it difficult to get rid of the annoying urine odor. Secondly, your pup will start enjoying the softness of the carpet and will want to poop on it instead of the paper. A spot in the laundry room, bathroom, or just outside the kitchen usually works well.

Covering the Area with Paper

Next, cover the entire room with puppy pads or newspaper. Set your dog's bed, a few of its favorite toys, and a water bowl at one nook of the room. Next, bring your puppy to this spot.

Let Your Puppy Take its Time

After your puppy is in the toilet area, let them take their time to excrete. Make sure to remove paper near where the puppy sleeps. Puppies have a natural instinct to avoid soiling their sleeping area. Therefore, if you remove paper from close to the bed, the puppy will avoid excreting in that area. Watch your pup closely and ensure it eliminates on the paper only. Every day, tear off some of the paper covering the room, so that you restrict your pup to defecate in one particular spot only. By the time you reach the seventh day, your pup would have perfected this technique.

Now that you know all the best and commonly employed dog training methods, you need to select one on the third day and start exercising it so you can train your dog to practice the method easily.

Positive reinforcement, encouragement, and conditioning will help you motivate your furry friend to obediently follow your instructions and make a proper habit of excreting in the designated spot. Let us discuss these methods in the next chapter.

DAY 5: CONDITION YOUR PUPPY - THE MAGIC OF POSITIVE REINFORCEMENT

You have selected, and started with a housetraining method. Now you need to ensure that your puppy obeys you and pays heed to all your commands, so he sticks to the method you chose.

To ascertain that, condition your dog to eliminate in the toilet area. To accomplish this goal successfully, you need the help of positive reinforcement.

Understanding Positive Reinforcement

Can you recall how your parents conditioned you to work hard at school? By giving you a few dollars or buying you a gift every time you got good results or by appreciating your effort, they showered their love on you in different forms whenever you did something good and that encouraged you to continue with that behavior.

This is what positive reinforcement is and exactly what you need to exercise with your pup. Positive reinforcement makes your furry baby obedient and makes practicing the housetraining methods we discussed earlier easier.

But you must adhere to the guidelines below so you employ the strategy the right way.

Correct Timing

Just as you must time when you show resentment towards your puppy when he does something wrong, you as well need to be very accurate with positive reinforcement.

You must reward your pup as soon as he practices good behavior. For instance, if you see him walking out the dog door as per your instructions, immediately reward or praise him. To ascertain that, observe your dog all the time.

Keep the Commands Short

Dogs cannot understand long sentences. Therefore, make sure to keep the commands short and clear when instructing them. For instance, avoid saying, "Billie, I want you to go poop in the litter pan." Instead, you should say things like, "watch me, stay, come, follow, sit, stand, off, leave it, go, poop" and similar short commands.

Be Consistent

Consistency is the key to positively reinforcing your dog to behave obediently and practice housetraining successfully. This is why you need to ask all family members to use similar commands, so your puppy does not become confused. In addition, everyone should be rewarding and unrewarding the exact desired and undesirable behavior, respectively.

When To Positively Reinforce Your Pup

Positively reinforce your doggie with treats and appreciation when she follows you to her toilet, and excretes properly, follows you back inside, eliminates on the right spot every time and goes in and out of the crate without creating any fuss.

Of course, you must use positive reinforcement when he or she performs any other good behavior; but here, our focus is primarily on housetraining. Make sure to avoid using positive reinforcement to shape bad behavior.

For instance, if you let your dog outside as a reward for being compliant with the housebreaking rules, don't let him out if he misbehaves. Your dog won't consider that as a punishment and will perceive it as a reward. Therefore, be careful when choosing reward and giving the reward to your dog.

Kinds Of Rewards

There're a variety of rewards you can use to condition your dog to practice good behavior and practices. These include, giving food treats to your pup, petting the pup, giving the pup a toy she loves, or indulging the puppy in his or her favorite game.

Note: Choose a treat or reward that entices your pet.

Your pet must not be able to resist that treat. An enticing treat will motivate your pup to continue obeying you in order to get the treat in return. Secondly, the treat needs to be small so your dog can instantly gulp and eat it. Don't give your dog a big biscuit or a bone because your dog will have to chew it, which will create a mess on the floor.

Also, avoid using meals as a treat. There needs to be a difference between a treat and a regular meal. In addition, keep a number of different small treats handy to ensure your dog stays involved in this practice and does not become bored of one particular treat.

In addition, appreciate your dog every time he follows a housetraining guideline successfully besides giving him the treat. Dogs love words of appreciation. Therefore, make sure to verbally praise your furry friend, try different rewards on your dog to find out which ones work best and only carry a few of the most effective ones.

Continuous And Intermittent Reinforcement

In the beginning, you should reward your pup each time he practices a certain potty training rule properly. This practice is referred to as 'continuous reinforcement;" it stimulates your pet to carry on with the good behavior. Once, your pup reliably and successfully learns a behavior, you need to switch from continuous to intermittent reinforcement wherein you continue with the reward, but gradually reduce its frequency.

In the first five to six days, you should reward your puppy with a treat each time he exercises a certain good housetraining behavior. After five days, reward her three of five times. Carry on with this for a few days and then reward her two of five times. Keep cutting back after every few days until you reward her occasionally. Intermittent reinforcement helps shape good behavior in your pup without making the pup greedy for treats.

Praise your dog each time he follows your command, but your appreciation can become less effusive than before. For instance, if you used to show extreme excitement and say lots of nice things to your puppy when she used to poop in the designated area, after a week, you should resort to 'good dog' only. However, you should show great excitement occasionally too so your puppy knows you are not angry.

Practice everything we have learnt in this chapter so you can correctly condition your pup to your chosen potty training method. Positive reinforcement will make your pup extremely obedient, so you won't have to worry about your entire house getting filthy with his piles and puddles.

DAY 6: USING THE STARTLE, BUT NEVER SCARE METHOD

On the sixth day, practice startling your dog when he misses an instruction or breaches a housetraining rule. Mostly, when you see someone going against your wishes or breaking a regulation, you tend to scare them with a shout or your loud tone.

It is likely that you will do the same with your pup when you see her pooping on the kitchen floor and not the newspaper. This act of scaring your dog is wrong and is likely to upset him instead of disciplining him.

On the sixth day, attempt to eliminate this behavior; instead, opt for the startle method.

How To Use The Startle, But Never Scare Method

Startling your dog means to make him or her attentive towards you to help the pup understand that whatever he or she is doing isn't right. If you see him peeing on the floor instead of the designated area, clap loudly instead of chanting his name loudly. The clap will startle him and make him aware of the wrong behavior. You could choose any startling gesture such as a snap of the fingers or a knock on the door. Make sure to stick to that gesture and practice it every time you find your dog disobeying you.

Be Consistent

Ask all household members to practice similar commands and rewards, and ask them to exercise the same startling gesture as well. If you clap at your dog when he pees at a different spot each time, then everyone else should clap at this behavior too. This helps your dog become conditioned to that gesture and understand that whatever she is doing is unacceptable.

Make Your Pup Practice the Right Action

After you have startled your pup, make him carry out the right practice and then reward him. This helps the pup know what he or she is supposed to do and the reward works as an incentive to make him continue with the good behavior.

DAY 7: PRACTICE ALL THAT YOU HAVE LEARNED

On the seventh day, carry on with all that you have learned in the past six days. You have decided on a potty training method, know your pup's routine, know what signals to look out for, and are aware of positive reinforcement, and how to use it; use these techniques to ensure your dog sticks to its schedule, and the selected housebreaking method. The seventh day is going to be easy for you because your dog will have grown accustomed to this regimen and would easily obey your commands.

By simply exercising the steps in this guide, you can train your dog to follow your instructions, defecate in the right are, help keep your house neat and clean, and keep himself tidy at the same time.

CONCLUSION

With the help of this guide, housetraining your puppy becomes incredibly simple. By following the effectual and beneficial techniques and methods we have outlined here, you can easily train your pup to pee and poop in the right spot every time; this will keep your house immaculate.

Implement this guide and experience amazing results in a mere seven days. Good luck. ☺

MY FREE GIFT TO YOU!

As a way of saying thank you for purchasing my book, I'd like to send you an exclusive gift that will help with using Dogs potty training.

Dog Potty Training is a quick and exclusive guide on how to potty training your dog in 11 steps. Check it out and bring the best version of yourself out NOW!

I am giving you this FREE BONUS to thank you for being such an awesome reader and to make sure I give you all the value that you deserve!

To get your FREE gift visit the link below and follow the steps & I'll send it to your e-mail right away.

maikon.leadpages.co/puppy-potty-training

Thank you again for purchasing this book!

I hope this book was able to help you to housebreak your puppy.

The next step is to implement what you have learnt.

Finally, if you enjoyed this book, would you be kind enough to leave a review for this book on Amazon?

Thank you and good luck!

PUPPY TRAINING

OTHER BOOKS BY DAN O'BRIAN

Dog Training: The Complete Dog Training Guide For A Happy, Obedient, Well Trained Dog

Made in the USA
San Bernardino, CA
31 January 2017